The Lawn Care Entrepreneur – A Start-Up Manual

The Ultimate Lawn Care Business Guide for the Gardening Tycoon

By Jamie Raines

Background

What motivates an individual to work for himself?

It is amazing how many people have deployed the phrase *'I've always dreamed of working for myself'* when they have lost their job. Very few people actually dream of working for themselves when they are young and many fall into self-employment rather than strive for it. Nevertheless, the question needs to be asked because entrepreneurship can only be learned to a certain extent but an entrepreneurial personality is something that you either have or not.

Let's put it very simply: when your business is doing well, working for yourself is the best job in the world - by far. However when your business is doing badly, working for yourself can be the worst job in the world - by far.

Scientific research has shown that it is your character and behavioural preferences which will determine how happy you will be if you become a self-employed entrepreneur.

So what does motivate you to want to work for yourself? The promise of unlimited earnings is certainly very appealing because when you're working for a salary, you are stuck with that payment and have absolutely no chance of making a fortune.

The real entrepreneur is the one who welcomes risk and thrives on it because, make no mistake, once you make that decision to work for yourself you are taking on quite a level of risk.

What are the dangers of starting a business?

I always remember many years ago someone telling me: *'I used to sell furniture... mostly my own!'*

Before I started my own lawn care business, I used to think that was quite funny, but after several years and especially remembering those early years, I finally understand exactly what he meant.

When you first start a business, there will be times when you experience negative cash flow and very often no cash flow at all. The test of any entrepreneur is the ability to deal with those early problems and all of them are to do with money, or should I say the occasional lack of it! Those are the times when you will recall how wonderful it was to expect a regular salary being paid into your bank at the end of every month.

If you are familiar with the phrase *'too much month at the end of the money'*, you will understand exactly what I went through and the purpose of this book is for me to pass on my experiences in the hope that they will lead you to success without making the mistakes that I made.

The rewards of running a business

Unless you are very lucky, do not expect immediate rewards as a self-employed person because you have to create your own wealth as it will not be handed to you by anyone else.

To an outsider one of the great attractions of self-employment is the fact that your time is your own and you're not subject to the regimentation of having to appear in an office at 9 o'clock every morning and leave at 5 o'clock in the afternoon. Your time belongs to you and because you're selling your time to a third party, your income is not dictated by others. You are the boss.

In practice, you will find that at the beginning, the hours that you put in will be much higher than they would have been if you had continued to work for someone else.

But that should not matter to you because most people who become self-employed choose an occupation which they are passionate about. If you actually like what you are doing, it makes the job much easier.

I found that one of the greatest rewards of running my own lawn care business was that I actually loved what I was doing and now consider my (quite substantial) income merely as a by-product of what I do.

Hopefully you too will experience that change in thinking.

Sourcing capital

Yes, money is important because without it you have absolutely no chance of success. The question is where to find the money to help you to start your business at the cheapest possible rate.

If starting a lawn care business has been your dream for some time, you possibly have saved a certain amount of money in order to give you that head start. If, on the other hand, you do not have any capital of your own, calculate how much you are likely to need for your equipment and living expenses and make sure as many people as possible know what your intention is. If you present a good case you may be surprised to find that both your family and friends will wish to invest in your company from the very beginning.

If you are lucky enough to own your own property, you may wish to think about liquidating some of the equity in order to provide yourself with some 'seed' capital. Remember those upfront expenses are extremely important because it is that initial cash which will give you that all-important first impetus.

Failing family and friends or savings, you may consider approaching your bank manager, although I do know quite a few people who took a major risk and funded their company start-up on a handful of credit cards. I'm not recommending that, but you know your own risk appetite!

One word of caution, before you actually even think about going to visit your bank manager or a third party who does not know you with a view to procuring some cash, make sure that you have put together a proper business plan and a cash flow forecast. I shall cover that later on in the book.

Limited company or sole trader?

Many people just start a business as a sole trader and eventually, when an accountant tells them to do so, form the business into a company and away they go!

My own personal experience was slightly different in that before I went into business, I made sure that I had a book full of orders and clients ready. I took deposits from some of the clients, diarised them a few weeks into the future and when my spade went into the first bit of ground, I am happy to say that I hit the ground running.

I did not put everything in place and then start looking for business. That brings me very neatly onto the title of the section. My own experience was that I had so much work lined up that I formed a company. That meant that the company was liable for any possible debts and if I had remained as a sole trader, I would have been personally liable for any trouble or any debts.

It is a matter of choice and largely to do with the volume of work that you expect to do and how quickly your business becomes viable and trading at reasonable volumes.

Thinking about transport

We discussed capital expenditure in the previous section and by far your biggest outlay is going to be for transport. I think it is important as even at this stage without proper transport you cannot possibly start a lawn maintenance business because in order to work, you are going to have to transport your equipment as well as soil, turf etc. and you cannot possibly do that without either having a van, a truck or at the minimum a car and trailer.

If you already have a van or a flatbed truck that is going to give you a very large head start but you may wish to consider a trailer. Also remember that you are going to have to be able to lift heavy items onto it. The worst possible thing that you can do is to start a business and in a few days later find that you have injured your back.

I'm going to cover transport in more detail in a later section but my personal experience was that a car, towing hitch and a trailer provided me with a great start.

The other reason I'm asking you to think about a vehicle at this stage is because it will form the basis of all your advertising. You cannot fail to have noticed that all vans and trucks have tradesmen's names and addresses and phone numbers on them. That is because when you are working and leave your vehicle parked outside the property, it is inevitable that people will walk past and those who may need your services will automatically be able to see that you're busy and at the same time they will have the opportunity to note down both your telephone number and your website. You can see therefore your transport is of major importance to your business but I will discuss that in much more detail later.

Boosting your specialist knowledge

As an amateur, it was enough for you to know certain aspects of lawn management but now that you're a professional, you need to be an expert. That means you need to know absolutely everything there is to know about lawn care.

When I started, I not only knew about every single type of grass and soil plus the optimum conditions etc. but I also knew about measurement, providing estimates for work, how to calculate prices, how to negotiate and the 1001 other things that you need in your head before you even begin to call yourself a lawn care entrepreneur.

It is all about giving yourself the best opportunity to make money and to give your prospective clients the right impression about yourself. If you hire a plumber or electrician or any other trade, you do not expect to ask a question and for them to reply *'I'll look that up or read about it and come back to you.'* You expect them to give you an answer immediately. Make no mistake, there are some clients who will ask you difficult questions which they already know the answer to just to check that you know what you're talking about. That means that you need to read every book you can on the subject, ranging from horticulture, marketing, laws and regulations to all the other pitfalls that you are going to come across.

Just as a guide, it took me nearly 6 months of study and learning before I was happy that I could face my first client. By the time I met my first client, I was able to give the impression that I had been doing this job for years.

Training

Are you 100% physically fit to do this job? If you spend an entire career sitting behind a desk, then you have to presume that you are possibly not as fit as you could be and although this section is not about physical training, it is well worth mentioning that you should make sure that your body is going to be able to stand what is an extremely physical job.

Every single book about gardening tells you to do a few stretching and warmup exercises before you begin any heavy work. I sincerely hope that you remember that and follow the advice. Your most important tool is your body and if it breaks even slightly, it costs you money. Eventually, once the volume of work coming in is such that there is very little gap between jobs, you will become fitter and fitter but nevertheless remember to do your stretching exercises and build it into your daily routine. This may sound like something very obvious, but you'd be surprised at the number of people who ignore the advice and end up with pulled muscles, strains, hernias and even worse.

The other type of training you need to think about, and not only before beginning a business but on an ongoing basis, is your own training within the field of lawn care and horticulture in general. Prepare yourself for the fact that when you go to somebody's garden to advise them on their lawn, there is a strange phenomena called the 'halo effect'. That simply means that because you are an expert on lawn care, your clients will assume that you are an expert on everything else within the garden.

Personally, I spent quite a long time working for a very small salary for a well-known garden maintenance company so that I could learn all the everyday tricks and knowledge that I knew I would need in my own business.

I would suggest that you give serious consideration to doing something similar, even if it means working as an unpaid intern. You'll be surprised how much more you can learn from observing than you can from books and the Internet.

Table of Contents

Questions to Ask Yourself before You Begin

Is Lawn Care Right for You?

Are you physically strong enough to undertake this job and are you willing to work in all weathers and possibly not work at all during very wet seasons? Do you have enough capital in order to take care of any downtime when you are not earning at all? Are you happy to work completely on your own without the security of a salary at the end of the month? Are you the sort of person who will be able to work physically all day and then come home and complete paperwork such as invoices etc.? Do you have enough marketing knowledge in order to 'kick-start' your business? Do you have the negotiating skills which are going to allow you to ensure that you are charging the correct price for the job? Are you motivated enough to work without supervision? Have you thought about doing this job part-time rather than breaking totally with your current job? Do you have the willpower to study in the evenings after you have completed the paperwork? **Not forgetting the more positive questions:** Are you looking forward to unlimited earnings which are directly proportional to the amount of effort you put in? Do you like the thought of being your own boss? Have you thought of employing people in the future and managing them?

Are You Willing to Spend the Required Hours to Make the Business a Success?

You are about to discover the difference between participating in the job and being totally committed to it. Yes I know that people who work for others claim to be committed to the company they work for but that is not real commitment because it can't be. When you are working for yourself and where your future and your family's future totally depends on your day-to-day effort and you don't know whether or not you are going to have enough money at the end of the month, you have to make sure that you are really committed.

There is no template or set of rules as to how hard you should work when you become self-employed but the rough guide is that you should be prepared to work for up to 16 hours a day. Remember that your job isn't merely digging and measuring. It is also telephoning, marketing, selling, negotiating, cash control, buying and all the many other items which make up the life of a self-employed business person. You should be prepared to get up at 6 am, work all the way through to 6 pm or later, then return home, clean up, eat and then do all the non-physical aspects of your work, starting with keeping your accounts up to date.

When Do You Launch?

It is not simply deciding on a month and a day on which to launch your lawn care business but more a case of deciding when you are ready. There are certain things which need to be in place before you even think of cutting your first blade of grass. The first is a solid business plan and cash flow. Second is enough capital to support you during any downtime and believe me, there will be downtime - especially at the very beginning of your venture. By the time you launch, you should know exactly what competition there is and how much they are charging. Your expertise should be 100% so that when you go and do your first estimate, you will be professional as well as realistic. You launch after you have acquired equipment and transport as well as insurances, not only for vehicles and equipment but also some form of liability insurance in order to protect your business. Your marketing plan should also be in place and of course there is absolutely no question of launching your new business without having clients lined up. Depending on where you are, there may be a few legal aspects that you need to know about ranging from starting a company, deciding on whether you prefer to work as a sole trader and even researching as to whether or not special permits are required for you to be able to operate as a lawn care specialist.

Do You Have Backup Capital?

There are two main reasons why new businesses fail. The first is that you are not seeing enough clients and secondly you don't have enough cash. One of the biggest dangers for the fledgling entrepreneur is some fanciful thought that once they get started in business, business will just keep coming. It won't. That is why you need enough cash in the bank in order to carry you through the lean months. Having said that and depending on your personal financial situation, you may be able to get away with simply having a credit card with enough balance on it to carry you through the bad times but you also have to remember that any debit balance on your card needs to be repaid. In my own case I always have enough spare cash to be able to live for three months without working. This sort of emergency cash is not merely for the times you are not earning but there will also be occasions when you have equipment emergencies for instance or there may be clients who are not happy to pay you a deposit in respect of materials and you may find yourself having to speculate through paying for materials yourself. Don't worry too much about that at this stage because in the long term, 'fronting' materials etc. can be quite profitable. The general rule is to have enough cash for 3 to 6 months. Yes it does sound like a lot of money, especially if you've never had 3 to 6 months' worth of cash but believe me from personal experience, you will function much better when you have a few thousand dollars that you can call on at any time.

How Much Do You Think You Will Earn?

You will not become a millionaire in the lawn care business until you are ready to employ people to do the work for you and then of course the sky's the limit. Remember there's a big difference between how much you are earning and how much profit you're making. You have to bear in mind that when you start a business there is an amount of capital expenditure which you have to build into your thinking. For instance if you buy a vehicle for say $5000, you can write that out of your books over a certain period of time.

What I mean by that is that you can decide that you will write off $1000 per year or say $100 per month towards your vehicle. That means that by the end of five years, your vehicle has been paid for. However, you do have to remember that if you earn say $2000 in month one that nets down to say $1500 if you take off your tax and expenses. You can carry out that exercise with all of your capital expenditure so that you can realistically calculate what your real income is. Later on, we're going to discuss how to cost jobs but it is well worth remembering at a very early stage that when you calculate what you are going to charge a client for the job, you do need to build in a certain amount for your standing costs. The question *'how much am I going to earn?'* is a very difficult one and the only true answer is *far less than you think* in the first two years – or until you establish yourself.

Conclusion

The lawn care business can be very profitable but not for everyone. We have already decided what the main two reasons for failure are, and assuming that you can override those, you can have a very long and lucrative career tending peoples lawns – and it is well worth remembering even at this stage that you are not limited to the domestic market and that there is also a very lucrative commercial market which you will no doubt wish to research at some stage. We will discuss this later, but I can tell you that personally I found the commercial market even more lucrative than the house-to-house market.

What you've read so far should give you the opportunity to realistically appraise whether or not this is for you. Remember the capital outlay, the equipment, the emergency fund, the insurances, the uncertainty, the seasonal nature of the work and the competition are all things that you should look at in a certain amount of detail in order to decide whether or not you wish to go ahead.

You should also look at your own personal motivation and ask yourself whether working for yourself is really something you wish to do. It is quite glamorous working for yourself but at the beginning it can be sheer hell – take my word for it.

You may already have the equipment and if you do, you have a head start with possibly very little to lose. But if you are starting with a blank sheet of paper no equipment and no cash, think about it very carefully. The most likely thing to happen to you is that you will find one or two jobs, complete them and then grind to a shuddering halt.

Hopefully you have not been put off by what you have read so far because it is a wonderful business to be involved in. Your choice now is to read on and learn how to get your foot in the door of a very enjoyable new profession or whether you stop here and maybe find something which doesn't require quite so much initial effort.

Step 1 – Planning and Analysing the Market

Competitors – Who Are They?

In theory, every single house or business with a lawn is a potential client of yours. However, the biggest competitors that you have are other people who wish to do the work themselves. Believe it or not, it is not impossible to persuade people that they could be spending their leisure time better than mowing grass and tidying their garden. It is much easier than you think. In fact, it is so obvious that there aren't many of your competitors who have thought of it. They're too busy advertising and waiting for clients to come to them. You may think that your main competitors are people exactly like you who are starting out on the lawn care business and dream of being multimillionaires.

Forget them. Half of them will fail in year one and of the remaining half another third will fail in year two. So that's most of your competition gone! Isn't it? Your competition are the franchisees, the landscapers, the so-called exterior maintenance experts, the professional gardeners.

You can see from their names that these are generalists but also remember that they are marketing themselves just as you are. You have the advantage of being an expert in a narrow field which will make you attractive to certain clients. The other people are real 'jacks of all trades' and as a specialist you should have absolutely no difficulty in dealing with them but only if as mentioned earlier, you become a real expert at lawn care, even before you start.

Many garden centres will run a maintenance business as a side-line and later on I will discuss how to do some of your marketing through garden centres and garden suppliers. The big advantage that you're going to have right at the beginning of your career is that your overheads will be low. Always remember that because it makes you competitive. So yes there is going to be a lot of competition, but if you box clever, you can ignore it.

Target Market

It is always good to have a target market because it will focus your mind. Let's start with dealing with your target market in a broad-brush sort of way and then we can focus down on specific groups. The target market is domestic lawn owners, commercial businesses and public authorities. By public authorities I mean any organisation which is paid for by the taxpayer rather than private enterprise. Local authorities look after parks etc. and yes I know that they have their own employees but trust me, there is business to be had even there — especially if you make a strong contact with whoever is in charge and sell yourself as the proper lawn doctor or lawn specialist.

Let's return to your domestic market. There is a group within that market who treat their garden like you might treat a gym. They believe that they need to be in the garden in the fresh air, spraining joints, pulling muscles and increasing the blood pressure all in the cause of health. That is quite a difficult group to persuade of the dangers of gardening - but there is one group which is quite amenable. The older gardener or more specifically the retiree gardener is an excellent prospect for you purely because of the fact that they have got to the stage where any job in the garden is hard work — that is why so many of them downsize so that they have a manageable garden. Nevertheless lawn care remains difficult for them. You are the solution to their problem.

In every area there are office buildings and industrial units. Very often, they have expanses of grass around their offices. You don't need too many clients like that to make a very nice living.

Budget

It is very difficult for a manual such as this to be too prescriptive as far as your budgeting is concerned because it will be read by people in different jurisdictions, different climates, different countries and different currencies. The best thing I can do therefore is to give you some sort of guide as to the items which you need to list and against which you need to put a number. When you have done that, together with adding an amount for what we call contingencies or a 'slush fund', you have a very good idea as to whether or not you want to start a business. If you do have some equipment that's fine but remember that you will need to maintain it, occasionally have it repaired and assuming that your business is doing really well, you'll be wearing the equipment out and having to replace it.

You're certainly not in need everything at once, apart of course from transport and a lawnmower, but you are certainly going to need things such as marketing costs, fuel costs and you should even think about things such as food and maybe even paying for the occasional assistant when your client has asked you not only to look after their lawn but to build a patio etc.

How to Write a Convincing and Realistic Business Plan

If you've never been in business and never written a business plan, you may find even the thought of this section extremely scary and that is why many business novices don't bother to do a business plan. There are many templates for putting together a business plan and what I propose to do is to once again do it broad-brush because different jurisdictions require different styles of plan. However there are certain sections and items which every plan needs to contain.

It is well worth mentioning at this stage that a proper business plan is not a cash flow forecast. A cash flow forecast is usually a fictional list of expenditures and income which you might wish to take to your bank manager in order to impress and persuade him to part with a loan for your business. It normally contains exaggerated income as well as unrealistic expenditure assumptions and as its function is purely to extract money from investors, I prefer to stick with the proper business plan... and on that note, do put together at least one realistic business plan and cash flow forecast if only to give yourself a realistic chance of building a proper business.

The normal business plan begins with an executive summary which tells the reader immediately what the business is all about. You should obviously state that you are in the lawn care business. It is also worth mentioning what you do in order to show that it is not simply a question of cutting grass. Include elements such as drainage, pest control, fertilisation etc. The executive summary should also contain an indication of what sort of legal setup you have. For instance are you a sole trader, a private limited company, a public limited company etc.? Whoever is reading your business plan should immediately see what you are up to.

Yours or your company's goals and ambitions should clearly be stated in the executive summary. You should also include a paragraph or two about yourself and your relevant experience so that people know who they are dealing with. Again it is important that you are truthful and keep exaggerations of your past achievements to a minimum!

Next you need to describe your 'financials'. Here's where the dreaded cash flow forecast raises its ugly head and the only bit of advice is the one I gave above which is to keep it realistic. A realistic cash flow forecast has far more chance of helping you to raise investment than some flight of fancy promising achievements which have never been previously achieved.

Unless you are very lucky, you are going to make a loss in year one. Nothing wrong with that, and that is what professionals expect. If your van, equipment etc. are all part of your business, it is unlikely that you will earn enough in year one to make a profit. Your cash flow may be good but your profit will not be good.

You have probably heard the term 'balance sheet'. Yes, accounting terms can be a bit scary but a balance sheet is simply a list of the assets and liabilities of your business as well as any capital. There are many pro forma available on the Internet which will help you to put together a realistic balance sheet. To put it simply, you list all your equipment, put a value against it and then on the other side you put all the money you owe.

Your business plan will also need to include a sheet of paper indicating your income and your expenditure. You may remember that I mentioned that you will not make much money in year one and if you include everything such as transportation costs, subscriptions, loan repayments, memberships, Internet fees, accounting, advertising, insurance, telephone, postage, bank charges and even tax provision, you can understand how what you may once have regarded as 'income' suddenly nets down to a much smaller figure. Once again, be realistic... and I should have mentioned that your own wages are also included in an income-expenditure calculation.

Your business plan will include not only your sales and marketing strategy but also a reasonably detailed analysis of the competition. Remember you are not working in a vacuum and you are surrounded by competition and your business plan ought to reflect what is different about you and what is going to make you succeed above others.

Finally, your business plan needs to have a look at the future and reflect the fact that you are aware that your ideas will constantly need to be revised and developed and you may wish to explore how your client bank is going to expand over the next say 3 to 5 years so that whoever is reading your business plan can see that you are thinking progressively and realistically. You may also wish to include any future employees and equipment purchases.

How to Plan a Marketing Campaign

If you are very lucky and you start your new business venture of lawn maintenance with a job or two under your belt, do not be tempted to ignore marketing. If you are not a corporate marketer, I shall simply tell you that marketing is simply telling as many people as you can about yourself and your business. It is far easier and more profitable to tell people about yourself and your services rather than sit back and expect people to come to you – because they won't.

Let's start with one of the great misunderstandings that non-computer literate people seem to believe. If you set up a website with your services on it, unless it is optimised in a certain way, you will not suddenly be hit with thousands of eager people wishing to look at your services and you. So don't be marketed-to by some clever web design company who will try to convince you that as soon as you have a website your fortune is assured. You need to develop a marketing strategy which involves many different ways of contacting your prospective clients as possible. Never ever rely on a single distribution channel.

For instance, many of your prospective clients are going to be in their 50s and 60s. Even now many of them do not automatically look for services on the Internet. That means that in order to attract people like that, you need to be thinking about more traditional methods of marketing such as pamphlets or possibly newspaper advertising or Yellow Pages. Brochures and flyers are an excellent start because they not only give lots of information together with possibly a rough idea of your prices but will also give you that air of tradition which is often appreciated by the older client.

Direct mail, whether by letter or email can also be very powerful but then again you're up against the whole question of unsolicited mail, whether paper or electronic. However, a small direct mail campaign can be very powerful, but bear in mind that if you are sending out 100 leaflets or letters, the response rate is always less than 1%

which means that you will possibly receive one enquiry. Now you understand why our post-boxes are constantly flooded with thousands and thousands of letters and leaflets. It's a very inefficient way of marketing but it can bring quite powerful rewards.

The first thing to do when planning a marketing campaign is to decide on two things. One, who you are going to be selling to and secondly, where you are going to be selling. There is little point in the blunderbuss approach whereby you send information to everyone. You may wish to start by targeting people you know or people they know. You may think about your local businesses and which of them could benefit from your services. Small newspaper ads are very cost-effective and in fact you should think about inserting a permanent small ad in your local newspaper or magazine.

By far the most powerful method of marketing and the one which you will gradually find helps your business to grow is what is known in the trade as the 'Referral Method'. That is simply where existing clients recommend you to people they know and it is by far the most powerful marketing method. Unfortunately, that is not something you can plan but it is something that will happen as a matter of course. The only downside of the word-of-mouth method of marketing is that it is very much a double-edged sword. If you screw up a job, it also tends to get around.

When putting together a marketing plan, do so before you actually launch properly. Not only decide on who and where but make a list of the methods that you are most comfortable using, enquire about the costs and then begin!

Free publicity is also very powerful. For instance in the context of lawn care, think about letting a local newspaper know that you are doing some freelance maintenance or garden maintenance in a couple of care homes for the elderly! You can even send in your own photograph and a short write-up. I've tried this myself and believe me it does work. Local newspapers are always greedy for copy and if you can give them something interesting with the human angle then so much the better.

The opportunities you have for marketing are so numerous that you really do have to think about which are the most cost-effective.

Survey Your Target Market

Your target market obviously depends on where you are situated but in general terms every person or organisation who owns a patch of grass is a potential client as are all those people who don't have a patch of grass.

It is well worth spending some time on something all budding entrepreneurs should do either physically or even figuratively - and that is to 'walk the floor'.

Decide on which area you want to work in and then get to know it. In fact, I shall give you a simple piece of advice which I've given to many entrepreneurs and salespeople before now and that is to use your own home as the centre of your area. Seems obvious doesn't it? However, you'd be surprised at the number of people who are ashamed to be seen by people they know, especially when they are in a new role such as this. Instead of using their own home and working outwards from it, they will choose an area away from their home so that they're not recognised. Believe me that makes the job far more difficult. You will not be surprised to hear that people who know you are going to be your best clients as well as the very best source of recommendations.

You can start to survey your target market by contacting people you know, family, former work colleagues etc. and write to them. Let them know that you are starting a new business, tell them what it is, include some sort of offer (if you wish) and if you're feeling cheeky enough, ask for the names and addresses of people that they feel could use your exclusive services.

In general terms and statistically, the people with the most money to spend are going to be people in their 50s and 60s as they are the ones who would have bought their homes 20 to 30 years ago and watched their homes inflate in value. Often they are the people without a mortgage and they do have disposable income. Try them first.

Personally, I also approached small building companies and the local authority who ran the area where I lived. They all proved to be very helpful so I suggest that you try that too.

Where Will You Be Based?

I trust that we've established that you need to be based where you live. That should be your very first choice, especially if you are in an area where you are known. Yes, I understand the argument that people may have known you for many years as say an IT expert and you may think they will find it very difficult to try and picture you as a lawn expert but the vast majority would admire your change of career and will be as helpful as they can.

One of the biggest fears of a new business is the safety of the equipment that you cannot possibly survive without. In short, you do not want your equipment to be stolen or damaged. If you are able to afford some sort of lock-up, storage or garage then you're very lucky. That is not available to every start-up and so you may have to be a little bit creative in where you keep your equipment.

If you have a van or some other form of transport, never leave your equipment in the van even if you are able to lock it properly. It is too much of a risk. You can of course compromise and only remove the most expensive items of equipment, especially overnight, but always be aware of security.

You may know someone who has a business of their own with lock-up facilities and there is no harm in asking them whether you can store your equipment with them.

When I started my business, I was living with my parents which meant that every evening I could offload my equipment and lock it away in the shed. Storage of your equipment should be part of your initial thinking, prior to putting together a business plan.

The likelihood is that no one is going to damage or steal your equipment but it's best to be as sure as possible (and insured!).

How to Minimise Start-up Costs

What are the big-ticket items that you are going to need to start a business? Obviously a decent lawnmower is somewhere near the top of the list, as is a petrol strimmer and maybe a rotavator. You may find yourself being asked to create a lawn with a path round it or through it. That may mean a concrete/cement mixer and maybe an angle grinder and various other bits and pieces. The good news is that you can hire most of these items and if you're very lucky, the hire company may have some pieces of equipment that it wishes to dispose of at a reasonable price. It's always well worth asking.

I started with second-hand equipment which I picked up from various yard sales and auctions and did all the maintenance and fixing up myself. As I am pretty risk averse, instead of buying a single lawnmower I bought two for what to me were quite obvious reasons in that if one broke down for some reason, I would not have to spend an afternoon looking for parts or trying to fix it. I had the second one available.

Earlier we talked a great deal about having capital available in order to be able to survive when there were down-times but a great way of avoiding having to have a lot of money is to do all your homework well in advance of launch, to the extent of having business set up and ready to go, maybe even before you buy your first lawnmower. A small amount of marketing legwork at the front end of the process, followed by enough bookings to take you forward say 3 to or 6 months means that you may be able to get away without allocating too much capital for the times when you won't be working.

That is what I did, and I'm passing it on to you.

What Is Your USP?

If you've already had something to do with sales and marketing, you know exactly what USP stands for? But if you don't, it means *Unique Selling Proposition* and that means possessing something which distinguishes you from the rest.

It doesn't have to be anything to do with the wonderful service you give, because everybody says that, but you need to get your creative hat on and think of something that is going to make you distinctive and more importantly, memorable.

This needs to be something that is going to motivate prospective clients to want to use you to do their lawn or more importantly something that is going to endear you to them and make them want to do business with you, no matter what it is.

You may decide for instance to spray all your equipment pink! Incidentally, I'm not for one moment suggesting that you do that but it's an example which would set you apart from the opposition because if someone referred to 'that guy with the pink equipment', even if they didn't remember your name, they would certainly be able to identify you. In this case it is nothing to do with service but it would be quite eye-catching – a USP!

Your USP could also be something like, for every two days you work, you will give or clients one day free.

One of those ultra-modern robot lawnmowers would certainly create a lot of interest and would be your USP.

Having a USP is all about differentiation so now would be a good time to sit down with a large pad of paper and get those creative ideas flowing.

My own USP was much less exciting than pink lawnmowers or topless gardening assistants... whenever I arrived on site, I would wear an immaculately clean and pressed overall with my name across the back and all my equipment would be clean and highly polished. Nothing exciting but believe me people did enjoy doing business with someone who looked professional rather than most of my competition who would rock up in torn jeans, dirty boots and a T-shirt.

SWOT Analysis

It stands for Strengths, Weaknesses, Opportunities and Threats.

The usual form of SWOT analysis is to simply take it piece of paper divide it into four sections and label each box with one of the above words.

The whole purpose of this exercise is to take a cold hard look not only at yourself and what you are able to provide but your environment and all the things that are going to stop you from being successful plus all the things that are going to insure that this new-found business of yours is going to be an immediate success. Let's have a look at a few examples under each heading.

Strengths: You may have had previous selling experience. You may have had previous gardening experience and if you work for someone else as an apprentice gardener or even if you help your parents in their garden, then that is another strength. You may have taken my advice and studied lawn care and are now an expert. You may have $10,000 in the bank as well as having bought all your own equipment - two more strengths etc. you get the idea.

Weaknesses: You are not used to working 10 hours a day. You have booked a three-month holiday. You don't have any proper transport. You know nothing at all about marketing. You have one lawnmower which keeps breaking down every 10 minutes. You need to learn about bookkeeping. You're going to need some extra help because you can't lift anything which weighs more than 20 kg etc.

Opportunities: There are three schools in your area and you are quite willing to cut their playing fields cheaper than the people who are currently doing it. You see that there are a lot of 'for sale' signs in the area which means future changes of ownership. There are several retirement homes in the area. All of them with very attractive grounds. As far as you know, you are the only lawn care service in town etc.

Threats: There are three other lawn care businesses within 5 miles of where you live. You don't think you have enough capital to take you through the first half year. It is almost impossible to advertise in your area and you're going to have to wander around distributing leaflets etc.

What I have written above are no more than examples. It is a very good idea for you to actually sit down and do a proper appraisal from where you are now and everything that is going to prevent you from being a success as well as all the positive things. You will find the SWOT exercise extremely helpful

Define Your Target Demographic

'Demographic' is one of those words which is more and more apparent but it is not always clear whether everyone knows exactly what it means. The official definition of Demographics is the *quantifiable characteristics of a given population.* Quantifiable means measurable and the 'characteristics' can be everything from education, nationality, religion, and ethnicity, through to age, homeowners, renters and even those who do or don't possess a lawn.

When starting up a new business, you could very easily waste a lot of time and money in leafleting or mailing people who would not require your services in one million years. So, studying the demographic is another way of focusing different parts of a population so that you are able to target the people who are most likely to give your business.

To make life simple, I would suggest that before you do anything else you have a good look at Google maps of your area. You can begin by establishing who has a garden and who has a lawn. That would be a very good starting point.

It is also very useful to know who the homeowners are and as I suggested earlier walk around to give yourself some idea of the age of the population, although that is another demographic which is a matter of public record.

Passing on my own experience, I can tell you that most domestic clients of mine are in their 50s and 60s and they all appear to enjoy a reasonable income. The income of a household is very important to you because you don't have to waste your time trying to market to people who are renting their home and live on a minimal income.

That is why it is important to get to know your area as well as you can and if, quite honestly, you don't have enough potential clients within your own area then you may have to look elsewhere, although from a logistics point of view working 'your own patch' is always the best way forward.

To summarise, choose a nice easy demographic such as people in their 60s who appear to have a reasonable income.

One point I would like to mention concerns big houses. New entrepreneurs and salespeople tend to have an aversion to large houses because they make assumptions such as 'they've probably already got their own gardener' or 'they probably won't respond to a direct approach'.

All I will mention on that subject is that my best clients all own very large properties and I approached all of them by knocking on their front door.

Franchising

No matter which jurisdiction you live in, I guarantee that there will be well established landscaping and garden supply businesses who will be able to help you to get yourself established. These are the people with a client bank who do all the marketing themselves and they will pay you to go and work on their behalf.

Usually to join any sort of franchise, you pay an amount of money in order to buy what is essentially a 'membership', the franchisee supplies you with tools and equipment and sometimes even transport and you work under their corporate umbrella.

If you are a red-blooded entrepreneur perhaps the franchise will not be suitable for you, but you should consider it especially if you don't have too much capital and are looking to acquire some experience.

Have a look in both the local and national press as well as the Internet for garden franchise opportunities and you will see how many of these are available.

Of course in years to come, you may find yourself in a position that your client bank has grown to such an extent that you yourself will need to subcontract or franchise back. Bear that in mind because once you have people working for you that is when your income really begins to take off.

Step 2 – Getting Your Business Set Up

Make It Legal

This is always a difficult item to think about for the young budding entrepreneur, because the temptation is always to begin by doing this type of work part time, while continuing with a 'proper' job, being paid cash in hand, not declaring it for tax and generally working slightly below the legal line.

The advice I would give you is to begin as you mean to carry on and that is to say, even if you begin by working part-time, you should begin to look like a professional by being able to produce an invoice and accepting payment either by cash, check or card.

At the outset, I said that I would not make this manual prescriptive in the sense that there is no right or wrong way to do most things – except when setting up a business. Your choices are limited.

If you decide to begin as a sole trader rather than any sort of company, you are able to accept cash into your personal bank account but of course that does have its complications from the point of view of extracting your payments or your outgoings from your normal household expenses. The good news is that if you do decide to start as a sole trader you can apportion parts of your household expenditure to your business. I'm not going to give you a long list but, for instance, if you have an office within your home and that can be just a laptop on the table under the stairs, you will be able to assume a cost for that deducted as a business expense. I suggest that you do some research and look at your local regulations as to how that might work well for you.

Whether you decide to start as a sole trader or jump in as a private limited company, I would suggest that you establish a separate bank account with its own debit card so that you can always see how your business is doing at a glance.

If you do decide to go the limited liability company route from the beginning, you *have* to have a separate bank account.

All you need to know at this stage really is that to begin a business and work for yourself is a very straightforward matter.

Also remember that from a marketing point of view, you will have much more credibility if you do arrive with your own headed notepaper, your own invoice book, bank account etc. For instance, if you have a sort code and bank account number at the end of your invoice, you can ask your potential client to simply transfer money straight into your account. Nowadays that is an instantaneous transaction and well worth thinking about. Much more impressive to your client then you insisting on cash.

Insurance

Yes, I know insurance is boring and I can already hear a big sigh as you prepare to skip this particular section!

Unfortunately, insurance is a necessary evil and it is there for individuals to protect themselves. Needless to say there is no such thing as free protection and it is something that you should budget for from the outset.

For instance, imagine you put a spade into somebody's garden and you accidentally cut right through a plastic pipe that takes mains water to their home. You now have a client without mains water and you have the possibility of an expensive repair and you don't have any insurance. What happens next? I'm not going to spell it out for you but unless you have proper insurance, you are endangering yourself and your business and as many will confirm, it's a great shortcut to bankruptcy if you don't have the capital available to put things right.

If you do have a lot of capital then it's not such a problem but you also need to know how much financial risk you could stand and then you should insure for an additional amount.

There are two main groups of insurance you need to think about. The first one is as mentioned above which is as a result of your negligence or incompetence or even your employees incompetence. That is insurance which covers your clients.

You will also need insurance to protect yourself against injury and you will also need insurance to protect your equipment, ranging from your vehicle, your equipment etc. as a result of damage or theft.

Needless to say, you will also need to insure your vehicle and make sure that you are insured for business purposes.

Nowadays it is possible to obtain a package deal which covers most of the above and the best place to go to for that is a properly registered insurance broker. Remember they work on commission and will be only too pleased to offer you advice!

Start-up Costs

Before you even begin to think about start-up costs, let's establish that your objective should be to minimise your start-up costs in order that you may begin making a profit as soon as possible.

The best way to get a rough idea of what your start-up costs are going to be, is to make a straightforward list and put numbers against each item. You can do most of this at your computer but if you want professional advice, go to an accountant who you know works for people involved in a gardening type business and they will give you a good idea of what to expect.

By far your biggest expenses will be transport, followed by your mower, your website, your office furniture, your telephone charges, your initial marketing and all the other tools that you are going to need ranging from edgers and trimmers to blowers and safety equipment.

There will be other items ranging from computers, dedicated cell phones, licence costs, maybe a PO Box number for your business address.

Your initial expenses are going to be as big as you want to make them or a small as you can manage to make them.

You may already have a mower and other equipment, you may be able to borrow them to start with... but whatever you do be prepared for the unexpected and that is why it is important for you to have some sort of fund available for things such as hardhats, steel toecap boots, even a pair of steel or aluminium ramps to get your equipment off your trailer etc.

If you want to add book cases, filing cabinets, desks, printers etc. then that is entirely up to you. But whatever you do, do not underestimate what you are going to need. There will always be surprises.

Stock

At the very beginning of your business life, you may decide not to carry too much stock because you believe that you will buy things as you go along. Yes it is very difficult to predict what you are going to need, but remember that when you're working for yourself the name of the game is to work continuously and try and anticipate all the things that will cost you time (and money). If you have to break away from what you are doing and go and stand in the shop or supplier's queue in order to buy a spark plug for your mower, a length of cable or weed killer you are costing yourself money.

If you do have a garage, shed or some other sort of storage facility, then it is well worth thinking about having certain items 'on the shelf' in order to minimise your downtime.

Think about spares for your mower because that is quite likely to be an important and major part of your equipment and the most likely to go wrong. Spare blades and drive belts are a good idea as is a spark plug and maybe a spare clutch cable. A can of two-stroke oil as well as a jerry can or two of fuel are also a good idea, but do make sure you are not breaking any regulations. As a matter of interest, I would have a plastic container of petrol for my mower and keep it outside.

Once again, decide on what type of work you are most likely to be doing and once you have costed the job and itemised the items you need, go and buy them in one go rather than driving to the supplier every day. If you know that you are going to need weed killer, calculate the amount and buy it, together with the means of dispensing it.

As a matter of interest, I make it a habit of having quite a few bags of various types of sand in store so that even if I do need extra, at least I can get on with the job while I'm waiting for a delivery. I even keep some concrete slabs as well as wooden planks and two wheelbarrows.

You know your business better than I and once again it is a question of you sitting down with a pen and paper and making a list.

It's all about anticipation and minimising your downtime.

Invoicing and Stock Control Software

One of the things that you are certainly going to be doing is invoicing your clients, not only for the time that you have spent with them but also the materials that you have paid for or even the materials that they have paid for in advance.

Most of the jobs that you will be invoicing will be on a fixed price because there are very few clients who would agree to take you on at an hourly rate – for reasons which are quite obvious.

To begin with, there may be times when through your own lack of experience you either undercharge or overcharge. Unfortunately at the beginning of your career you are far more likely to undercharge but as time goes on, you will learn what the job takes and believe me you will be a great expert at quantity surveying!

An ideal situation is for you to develop a 'circuit' of clients that you visit at least say once a month and people like that, can be put on a monthly bank direct debit so that you know that a basic amount of cash is coming to you on a regular basis

If you are selling to the demographic that we discussed above, that is to say those in the 50+ age group, believe it or not they do appreciate a paper invoice.

As a tradesman, I would suggest that you start simply by having a rubber stamp made with your name, the name of your business and telephone number, together with your address and website.

That means you'll be able to buy a generic invoicing book, and simply stamp each page with your details. That is the sort of invoice that many people expect from a tradesman and it also means that you don't have to go to the hideous expense of having headed notepaper printed at the front-end of your career.

If you are not dealing with a regular client, invoice immediately the job is completed. There is absolutely nothing wrong with someone in our business producing a handwritten invoice. In fact from a marketing point of view it is rather nice for someone to see a handwritten invoice rather than a sterile looking machine typed one.

However, once you get to the stage where you have to produce quite a few invoices every month, allocate a day per month for invoicing and general administration. Yes you are baking in a postage cost as well as stationery costs but that does give a certain professional image once you are a proper business rather than a sole trader.

Will You Need an Assistant?

At the very outset, you will not have the ability to pay for any employees but there will certainly be times when you need somebody on the other end of the heavy piece of equipment or someone to help you to speed up a job.

In the absence of a full-time assistant, you should have two or three people that you can call on at short notice to come and help you.

The worst thing in the world is for you to walk away from a job and have to refuse it because it has to be done quickly which means that it needs more than one person or it may involve a little bit of heavy work which again cannot be done by a single person. It is very difficult to turn work away, especially lucrative work just because you can't manage to do it.

Let's just say that although you will always be able to find someone to help you, it is best if you have someone that you know and trust. You do not need to hire an Einstein because, let's face it, the jobs that you are most likely to ask them to do is either to hold the other end of something heavy or possibly mow some grass , cut some weeds or dig.

If you do hire someone else, do make sure that your insurance covers them because the last thing you want is for someone to injure themselves whilst working for you. It doesn't matter if they hurt themselves through their own negligence, the most likely outcome is that the liability is yours.

The other thing I'd like to mention as far as hiring others is concerned is that you need to make sure that you do build that expense into any estimate that you produce for your client. When you are quoting for a job, always think as to whether or not you are going to need help because if you don't allow for that in the initial figures, you could find yourself with severely eroded profits.

If you genuinely have no idea where to look for casual labour, try Facebook or Twitter or even the local press.

Employing others is well worth thinking about right at the outset because there will definitely come a time when you are employing people full-time so you might as well get your practice in early!

Step 3 – Getting Equipment and Learning How to Use It

The Mower

Needless to say, if you are a lawn care specialist, a lawnmower is going to be piece of equipment which is going to earn you your income. As you have probably already discovered, the number of various lawnmowers on the market is massive which means that you do have to be careful when choosing what is going to be the nucleus of your entire toolkit.

Personally, I started and continue to use a petrol mower and I have always chosen a self-propelled mower. They tend to be little bit more expensive than the push along type but are well worth investing in.

The difference in cost isn't all that vast but be careful when purchasing one because pushing a petrol mower full of grass cuttings is very tiring and a mower which has driven rear wheels will make a huge difference to you.

There is a difference in quality between domestic mowers and commercial mowers because domestic mowers are not expected to last many seasons. You need to have a mower which is built robustly enough to last you a long time and at the same time be reliable.

There is absolutely nothing wrong with the domestic mower, but I suggest that you spend a little more on your main machine. Start with something which has, say a 24 inch cut and have another machine – a domestic one is fine – as a backup.

There may be occasions when you need the comparative quiet of an electric mower. I've only come across that once and that was a job we had to complete around an old people's care home where we needed a comparatively quiet electric mower.

One of the things that you'll soon discover is that mowing grass produces waste. Before you start cutting, make sure that you have somewhere to dispose of the cuttings. Be prepared for the fact that there may be times when you have to take them with you. Whatever you decide, make sure that you discuss it with the owner first. Obviously a compost heap is by far the best solution for you.

Hedge Trimmers

You may be wondering why there is a section on hedge trimmers within a manual on lawn care. A petrol or electric hedge trimmer is a comparatively cheap piece of equipment and you can even pick up a pre-used one in reasonable condition.

I guarantee that if you turn up to cut somebody's lawn, there will be occasions when you are asked to do several other jobs and it is best to be prepared. The last thing you want to do is for your client to call somebody else to do their hedge and then for them to discover that the person doing the hedge can also do lawns. Be prepared to do everything.

Trimming hedges is a comparatively simple job but as far as a hedge trimmer is concerned, there are masses of possibilities which include the old-fashioned hand shears. Do not ignore those because there will be times when they are very useful especially in smaller gardens.

What you're looking for is an item of equipment which will produce the best possible job in the fastest time. You may find that you buy a hedge trimmer and you don't use it for a very long time but is still worth having.

Once again passing on my own experience. I bought to hedge trimmer second-hand from a well-known Internet auction site (yes that one!) and have found it very useful and reliable.

The reason I bought my equipment second-hand to start with this because I wanted commercial quality trimmers rather than the toy ones that you find in DIY stores. The non-commercial ones tend to be either too flimsy or far too heavy for commercial use.

Finally, I suggest that you buy a double-edged trimmer because they enable you to complete the work much faster than a single edge.

Another recent innovation which I think is worth mentioning is the hedge-trimmer with a telescopic shaft which will enable you to reach high hedges. From a safety point of view this is much safer than standing on a ladder.

Edgers

In this section, I am going to express a personal preference as far as edging a lawn is concerned. I do all of my lawn edging by hand using a half-moon cutter. Yes there are some excellent commercial edgers which are usually motorised and on four wheels and they do an excellent job. I have tried them but have never the less found that for 95% of the work that I do, I can obtain a perfect finish by hand.

So, unless your first contract is a 2 acre lawn for a golf course, I suggest that you wait before you invest in the motorised edger and do the work by hand. The Half-moon Edger is basically a spade and in fact a well-sharpened spade would also do an excellent job.

You can also buy modern combination tools which are basically strimmers with an edge attachment. These are very good for your own garden but for heavy duty commercial work, stick to the purpose-built edger or my preferred hand method.

In case we're talking at cross purposes, the next section is about strimmers or trimmers (depending where you come from). They just cut the grass at the edge of the lawn, whereas a proper edger actually removes pieces of soil.

Once again, I would remind you about the waste that you, the contractor will have to deal with. If you have edged quite a reasonably sized lawn, you may be left with quite an appreciable amount of soil and grass to dispose of. You can either take it away with you or preferably dig it in somewhere in the garden.

It may sound obvious but I have found that one of the most important pieces of equipment to have as part of my edging arsenal is a very long piece of string on two sticks which is an invaluable aid to creating a straight edge. Otherwise, use a builder's plank or two. Trying to cut a straight edge by eye is possible but not until you've had a lot of experience.

Strimmers

Just to clarify what I mean by a strimmer, it is the piece of equipment which has a rotating head and usually a length of strong nylon string or rope which acts as a cutting-edge. It is extremely useful for parts of the lawn that you cannot reach with a lawnmower. For instance a lawnmower can only cut to within a few inches of a wall and it cannot cut right up to a tree and that is where the strimmer comes in.

Once again, my own preference is for a motor driven strimmer. They usually have a small bracket (50 cc) two stroke engine, they start with a pull cord and are extremely reliable.

There are also many electric versions of the strimmer but for commercial use, use a petrol one. This is one piece of equipment which you can buy second hand in the full knowledge that it is most likely to be working perfectly well. It is the sort of equipment that people buy, use once and then forget. Personally I don't use an electric strimmer purely because of the inconvenience of long lengths of cable. However there are now rechargeable strimmers which is yet another option for you to try.

If you have a properly solid professional strimmer, you can usually interchange the head which contains the bobbin of nylon string for a single blade, usually called a brush cutter. These are very useful when you come across a garden where there is a lot of weed or dense undergrowth or even a mixture of grasses and weed which needs an initial 'blitz' before using a lawnmower.

Look out for a strimmer with a rotating head which can be used to walk along and edge a lawn.

I have not included this in a separate section on safety equipment but I do suggest that whenever you're using a strimmer, that you wear protective goggles. I'm only mentioning this from personal experience because there will be times when you will inadvertently hit a stone with the strimmer and you can imagine the consequences if you are very unlucky.

Once again from a safety point of view, do remember that if you do decide to use an electric strimmer or electric mower, do not plug it straight into the mains but do so through a trip switch so that if there is a problem, your machine trips-out at source without electrocuting you.

Equipment Guarantees

It is quite surprising how often people buying expensive equipment don't bother to fill in the guarantee card or keep the receipt in order to retain proof of purchase should the machine go wrong.

Firstly, if you are buying a new equipment, register the guarantee and place a guarantee card or letter somewhere accessible, preferably in a guarantee folder. Yes I know that sounds obvious but as an amateur it didn't matter but as a professional, it is absolutely vital not only that your equipment is fixed but that it is fixed quickly.

Luckily though, modern motors are built to such a high standard that you are genuinely very unlikely to have any problems. Once again it's all a question of how much risk you are willing to accept.

Whenever you do have a piece of equipment fixed by a professional or even serviced, do ask for how long it's guaranteed. It will usually be for three months. That may not sound much but it could be very useful to you. The last thing you want is to have your lawnmower fixed and on the following day have to take it back and start again.

When you are in a start-up situation, that is of course the advantage of buying new equipment rather than second hand – the guarantee. However when you are buying second-hand, you are buying at a lower price so if you buy at the right price, the risk is well worth it.

Fuel Storage

The first thing I will say about fuel storage is DON'T! Certainly not in any quantity. Petrol fired mowers and strimmers are quite efficient and fuel is not going to be one of your major overheads but neither is it a zero cost.

It is one of those things that you need to build into your thinking when quoting for a reasonably size lawn so do make a point of remembering roughly what sort of area of lawn you can cut on a full tank. I'm not suggesting that you should show it as a separate item on your invoice but do remember your fuel costs which incidentally should include your travel costs when assessing a job.

Personally, I have a 20 L petrol tank which I store outside my shed and which is there purely for emergencies.

However, I do have a store of 2-stroke oil as well as normal engine oil but once again we are only talking of a couple of litres so it is not a major amount.

It is a good idea however for you to carry a couple of cans with you at all times so that when you do go and fill up your van or truck, you can keep your small cans topped up.

There's nothing worse than running out of fuel halfway through a lawn and then having to look like a rank amateur by getting in your car or van and driving to a petrol station in order to fill up a can.

Hand Tools

Put yourself in the shoes of those lawn care specialists of a couple of hundred years ago – before the days of even push along mowers and certainly well before the days of petrol and electric mowers plus the myriad of all other gadgets and tools that you have access to.

In those days, everything was done by hand – yes even those manicured lawns were done by a real specialist with the razor-sharp scythe.

I have to admit that I have had the privilege of watching one such expert cutting a football field by hand and it was a very impressive sight... and you may think that all those ancient tools are well and truly buried and no longer in use.

I also have to admit that I'm a great fan of hand tools and even now sometimes find that a sharp sickle can be very useful in cutting weeds and as I mentioned earlier my personal preference is for lawn edging by hand.

Just because you have an electric hedge trimmer and a strimmer does not mean that you should forget all about hand shears, long handled and telescopic handled shears, clippers and all the other bits of hand equipment. On the contrary I would suggest that you go out and collect a reasonable collection of all of those because you will find them useful.

There are occasions when I still use long handled right angled shears to trim a lawn. There are also times when it is much quicker to pull out a pair of well sharpen shears in order to cut a small hedge – especially if your petrol hedge trimmer refuses to fire up the some reason.

You should not ignore hand tools because they are a fabulous backup. They mean that even if all of your modern motorised and electrical equipment breaks down or refuses to work, you can still earn money. I have one business acquaintance who still swears by a non-motorised push along mower for some very fine lawn cutting. It is all a matter of personal taste.

The one thing I will say about any hand tools, including forks and spades which you should also have as part of your arsenal, is not only to buy the best possible tools that you can afford but to clean them and look after them and in the off-season to clean them with an oily rag or spray them with WD-40. In other words if you are not using them or they are going to be standing for a while, make sure that they don't rust or spoil.

From a marketing point of view, you will find that all your clients will find it very impressive if they see that you are still using hand tools occasionally.

A Vehicle

Don't worry, I'm not going to recommend any specific vehicle because there is no right and wrong answer but it is the most important piece of equipment, apart from your mower and it is well worth thinking about how you are going to transport all your equipment, bags of sand, bags of peat, bags of gravel etc.

My own preference is a station wagon which is quite roomy and good for storage plus a trailer which will take all of my mowing and cutting equipment as well as being useful for transporting rubbish away from the site or bringing sand etc. to a site.

However, I do have a lock-up garage into which I can reverse my trailer and leave it secured overnight.

Maintain a healthy pair of aluminium ramps which are not only used to push equipment from the trailer to the ground but I also have been known to use the ramps on site to push a wheelbarrow along solid ground etc. That is what suits me but may not necessarily suit you.

One could argue that the most useful piece of equipment would be a small flatbed truck or lorry with either a winch or a tipping mechanism... but let's face it that would be a very expensive outlay and do not feel pressured into spending several thousand dollars on such a vehicle unless as I said earlier, you have already booked a few hundred thousand dollars' worth of contract before you start.

You are not going to need to transport tons of topsoil to a site and have to unload it, well certainly not at the beginning. However, if you are able to obtain finance in order to enable you to purchase such a piece of equipment, by all means go for it! Personally, I have found that I am able to function extremely well with a station wagon and trailer and have only very occasionally had to hire larger equipment because nowadays most suppliers will deliver to your site.

My name and contact details are on my station wagon and I have opted for magnetic signs which I can take off but you can pay a sign writer to do a more permanent job on your vehicle and of course now we have the modern option of stick-on decals which are very reasonably priced these days.

Whatever you do, do not attempt to do any sort of signwriting yourself. It will cost your business. You do not want to be perceived as an amateur even before you make it through your potential client's front door.

Purely as a matter of interest, I have decided that my ideal configuration will be something like a Land Rover plus trailer. I'm only mentioning that in order to give you more food for thought.

There is another vehicle which you should remember and should have as a standard piece of kit and that is a wheelbarrow. Buy the best wheelbarrow that you can possibly afford because you will find it the third most useful piece of equipment after your van and your lawnmower. Everything from your lawnmower to your tools and topsoil can be transported in a decent wheelbarrow.

Storage Premises

Storage premises come in all sorts of shapes and sizes from purpose-built premises and workshops to prefabricated buildings and sheds to somebody's spare garage. Once again, there are no rules but do try make sure that whatever you decide on is secure and another reminder is to make sure that all your equipment is insured against theft – and it will only be insured against theft if the premises where it is stored in are secure.

I started with a shed and if you are to back me into a corner I would suggest that you invest in a shed and a large padlock. You can fit out the interior of the shed as you like but make sure it is big enough to take all of your equipment including your mower(s).

If you are lucky enough to have a garage, all you need to do is fit some of it out with shelving and you have an instant storage facility.

Personally I feel much more comfortable if I know that my equipment is not too far away from me but if you are happy to rent or buy a storage facility away from where you live, then by all means do so... but do make sure that it is secure. However, unfortunately it is another expense which you will have to build into your budget.

Yes, you do need a storage facility but right at the very beginning of your venture, remember that you also need to keep your expenses as low as possible. If you do not have the capital for a shed, by all means ask around and I am sure that you will find an unused garage somewhere in your area and if you can use it in exchange for doing that person's gardening, then everybody wins.

And also remember that any storage facility needs to be pretty high up on your list.

Equipment Hire

At some stage, we have all had to hire some equipment. As an example the last thing that I hired was a mini digger which I needed to cut trenches in order to install a drainage system underneath the lawn. That is a very good example of the sort of equipment which you should hire rather than have sitting around 90% of the time doing nothing.

However there may also be times when your own equipment breaks down and the faster solution is for you to go immediately to your local supplier and hire say a mower. If you recall that is why I suggested that you have two mowers so you can always be guaranteed of having at least one that is working.

But having said all that, everything that you can possibly think of is available for hire right down to a spade and fork. For obvious reasons, that is not the sort of equipment that you should be hiring unless you are happy to constantly eat into your profit margin.

If you can buy equipment which is pre-used but which is in good condition or that you can have serviced then by all means do so. I'm a great believer in being over-equipped – which means having two or three spades instead of one, two strimmers etc. that means that I only need to visit the hire shop when I'm either desperate or when I need to hire a piece of specialist equipment.

For instance when you are lucky enough to have obtained a big job, you may need to transport soil, bricks etc. and it may be an idea for you to hire a dumper truck or even a tractor and grass cutter for when you blunder into that contract where you have to cut 20 acres of grass. It will happen!

So save all your equipment hire activities for the times when you have absolutely no choice.

I own a rotavator which I managed to buy for a very reasonable price and which I thought would be very useful and welcome addition to my tool chest. I have used it three times in the last two years and usually only start it just to check that it is still working. That is a fine example of equipment that you should lease… at least until your workforce and jobs are measured in double figures!

Step 4 – Advertising

Choosing an Attractive and Memorable Name for Your Business

If you are operating your business as a sole trader, there's absolutely no problem or issue with working under your name with a strapline underneath the name describing exactly what it is you do.

There are some schools of thought which will tell you that you should spend a lot of time and money on choosing the right name for your business but the fact is, it will not be until you're generating enough income to become incorporated that a business name really matters.

The advantages of using your own name is that people you're dealing with will immediately know that they are dealing with the boss. The downside is that they will also know that you are a small business and that you are unlikely to be able to take on larger contracts – but when you first start that will not be an issue.

So, unless your name is not suitable as a business name, for example, if my name was "A. Crook", then I would think twice about using it for any type of business! However, most names look perfectly reasonable, especially if underneath you had something like 'grass expert' or 'lawn care specialist'. Do not get hung up on the name and certainly at this stage, you should not be paying someone to brainstorm a 'suitable' name.

And please do avoid those hairdresser type puns such as 'Cutting Remarks', 'Jack the Clipper" etc.

If however you are set on choosing a name for your business, make it look respectable and solid. For instance, 'The Lawn Care Company' is much more solid than 'The Lawnmower Man'.

If you decide on a name, register it. If you decide to form a limited company, it will also help you to make sure that no one else is operating under your name. You wouldn't want to upset the tax authorities would you?

Logo for Your Business

Let's face it, a lawn is not the easiest thing to express in a logo but when choosing a logo it is important to realise that it is eventually going to become a part of your corporate image and that is why companies sometimes spend fortunes on logo design.

As you are probably in the start-up situation, do not waste too much time or money on logos because if you go on line, you will find any number of logos which will be appropriate to your type of business. However, if you do choose a logo online from a logo site, be prepared for the fact that hundreds of other people will be using that same logo.

A logo does not have to reflect what you do. Look at McDonald's, their logo is instantly recognisable even though there isn't a burger in sight.

You can easily reflect what you do by say a picture of a lawnmower, shears or any number of quickly recognisable lawn care and garden tools.

There is absolutely no harm for you to have a logo which perhaps expresses a more general gardening 'feel' than a purely lawn related one. After all, if my own personal experience is anything to go by, you are most likely to end up doing a whole range of gardening work.

Take your time when choosing a logo because eventually it'll become the most identifiable part of your company.

Your logo does not have to be a picture. One of the most popular and classy types of logo are of the typographic variety. These logos are just text or perhaps a symbol.

Abstract graphics are also just as powerful as an illustrative logo.

The reason I'm trying to highlight the above is because you don't have to limit yourself to gardening equipment and flowers when thinking of a logo.

Remember that your logo is not going to change every few weeks. Your logo should last you a very long time and if you think of all the well-known logos that you see every day, you will also realise that they have been with you for a very long time.

You need to ask yourself several questions when designing a logo ranging from who you are trying to impress to how you are going to differentiate yourself from all the other lawn care specialists and of course your logo should somehow fit in with your motto or tagline.

A very good starting point is to look at some of your more successful competitors – in a research rather than the plagiarism sort of way!

You may be interested to know that 95% of the top logos in the world only use two colours. The most popular colour is blue and the second most is red. That means that you do not have to limit yourself to green, although in the logo world green is known to represent nature, good health and peace. Browns and greens tend to be associated with wealth and prestige.

Many companies use blue as their main colour because that subliminally suggests strength. Red is all about energy, aggression and action.

I have devoted a few more words to logos then I normally would but I'm just trying to express that a logo is quite important to the success of your business and the image that you are trying to convey.

Business Cards

If you do your marketing properly, you should get through quite a few business cards. Go to any garden centre shop and you will probably find a stand somewhere containing piles of business cards from various tradesman, including lawn care specialists.

Look at each one of those cards and the design and without even knowing what the tradesmen or company are like, you will immediately derive some sort of mental image of what they are like. Yes it sounds ridiculous but unfortunately it is true.

In the same sense when you speak to someone on the phone, you immediately create a mental picture of what they look like. Yes, most the time it is wrong but nevertheless we all go through that process.

There are many standard card designs which you can once again find online. Most of them are absolutely awful and can be far too gimmicky.

When deciding on a business card, think about the people you want to be doing business with. If you are aiming for the 50+ group or the corporate market, your card needs to be sober, simply the description of what you do and your logo.

Forget jokes, funny pictures or complicated design. Go for the simple clean look and make sure that your telephone number and email address are clearly visible. I have seen far too many business cards with far too much design in them where the important bits such as the telephone number and email address are being constructed in what looks like 3pt Times New Roman which makes them almost illegible.

Put your name on the card and please do not give yourself a fancy title such as chairman or managing director. Proprietor is good.

If you have relevant qualifications or even non-relevant qualifications whether or not you put them on a card is entirely up to you. There are some people who absolutely adore to see letters after someone's name but my personal taste is to leave them out.

On a personal level, I used to work for an American company and for a while was based in the United Kingdom. I had two sets of cards: one with my first name and surname across the middle for the American market and another set with my initial, surname followed by degrees and various other nonsense.

The market that you are in means that what is most important is your ability to convey your experience rather than qualifications. However if you do have a relevant qualification or maybe a degree just put that but avoid putting any more than one thing after your name. Contrary to popular belief, you will be impressing no-one!

My own favourite colour for a business card is black on white with a logo, although in the same way that blue conveys trust and dependability on a logo, it also does that on a business card.

Navy Blue

If you want to become a cliché, by all means have your card printed in green with a little lawnmower in the corner!

Shirt

I fully realise that a personalised shirt is not the number one item on your marketing list, but nevertheless if you do have the capital it is always worth continuing to develop your corporate image by having a shirt with your company name and phone number on the back and possibly the logo on the front.

Right at the very beginning of your business, this could come under the heading of unnecessary expense but as your business gains momentum you will find that even a T-shirt with all your details on used as a 'giveaway' will be much appreciated by your customers.

I have T-shirts all in 2XL with my contact details on the back and a motto on the front which is a joke about grass. Whenever I present someone with an invoice, they get a T-shirt. Very small gesture and extremely appreciated by most people.

However, this is not something you should get hung up about right at the very outset of coming into the lawn care business but nevertheless it is something to bear in mind and whether it's a T-shirt, a hooded top or a baseball cap, it can be a very good addition to your marketing effort.

The only thing I would further mention about shirts is that if you have people working for you, do make sure that they wear your corporate shirt and if you're going to be in the habit of giving them away, ensure that they are of the best quality that you can afford.

The last thing you want to be giving away is cheap tops or T-shirts which become the size of a postage stamp when they have been in the wash the first time. As far as clothing is concerned I would rather not distribute cheap quality items. You would be far better off with other marketing material such as pens, notepads etc.

Lawn Signs

We're still discussing advertising or in this case more precisely, name recognition signs, otherwise known as yard signs, placards or name boards. They are very much favoured by estate agents (real estate agents, realtors) and they are the rectangular or plastic signs you see outside people's houses. They are usually on a wooden pole and either tied to the front gate or hammered into the ground.

Name recognition is going to be very important for your business and if you can get away with having say, a dozen of the signs made up, and distributed amongst your friends who are willing to hammer them into the ground in the front garden, then people will see your name and telephone number and in general, this method will generate clients for you.

You should be aware of the fact that in certain jurisdictions, you need a licence to put up signs like this but certainly use one while you are working on the site. It will help you if your name and contact details are clearly visible to passing motorists and pedestrians.

If you are a real estate agent, what you put on the sign is very straightforward. Your contact details, your phone number and either 'sold' or 'for sale'.

My personal preference is very straightforward. I have a board with my details, what I do with contact details. Instead of the addition of a 'sold etc.' addition to the sign, I have 'lawn created by' along the top of the sign. I can tell you that has been very successful, especially if I'm working in the front garden where people can stop and have a quick chat with me.

There are quite a few companies who can make these. They are inexpensive and well worth investing in, as are a dozen or so sharpened 2" square wooden stakes.

Believe it or not, lawn signs are a very effective form of cheap advertising and well worth looking into.

Flyers

Flyers are the single sheets of paper that are delivered by the postal authorities. They tend to be in colour and have lots of detail about an organisation and its products. They are very cheap to produce and have to be distributed in quite large numbers because the response rate on those is of the order of 1%. That means that you will have to distribute about 100 of these in order to achieve one response. Having said that, a single response is quite likely to pay for the entire campaign.

Wherever I'm working, I make a point of distributing flyers not only in the road that I am working but also to several roads within the vicinity.

Flyers, handbills, circulars or whatever you'd like to call them can be produced roughly $20 per thousand although of course that cost does vary but it does give you a rough idea of what you will be investing.

It is not a very effective form of advertising but nevertheless anything that can increase your client bank would be worth doing especially if you can do it at minimal cost.

If you Google 'flyers' you will see a vast number of websites who will print them for you and a lot of them have ready-made templates into which you can insert photographs as well as text.

I have found that the most effective flyers are the ones with the least information on. There are far too many flyers where the company owner is trying to include far too much information. Usually, anyone receiving a flyer will look at it and if it doesn't appeal, they will bin it, especially if one side of the flyer contains 1000 words of closely packed text.

Keep your message short, include your name and address and a bullet point list of what you do, distribute them, sit back and wait.

A4 Flyers are also very useful because they can be attached to the backs of any letters of correspondence.

Once again on a personal note, I have had my name address and a few details of what I do printed onto magnetic strips for prospective clients to put up on their fridge with all the other magnetic bits and pieces. That is a slightly more expensive approach than paper flyers, but they do have the advantage of being constantly visible, useful and less likely to be headed for the bin as soon as they are posted through the letter box.

Whatever you do, do not attempt to print your own flyers using your own printer with a flyer template you have found somewhere on the Internet. It will give any prospective clients exactly the impression you do not want to achieve.

Create Your Own Website

I say 'create your own website' but I do so with one proviso – make sure that you at least vaguely know what you are doing. If you are not HTML-savvy you will find that there are thousands of website templates out there and all you need to do is provide the photographs and the copy.

However, if you're not very good at writing or describing what you do, it is well worth asking a professional to write the words for you. There's nothing wrong with that. We all have our individual skills and in the same way that somebody can come to you as a lawn expert you can go to another person who is a copywriter.

Copywriting is a perceptively difficult art and commercial writing of this nature is designed to motivate a potential client to choose you over the hundreds of other suppliers that you may be competing with. Once again, the best starting place for you is to read and study the websites of people in a similar business to yours.

You've probably heard of WordPress which is blogging software. This should be more than enough for the type of business that you are going to be operating in.

As far as the content is concerned, put yourself in the potential clients place and ask questions that you would expect to be answered. The client needs to know things such as who you are, how long you have been a lawn care expert and how much you charge. Those are the three basic things which you should ensure are mentioned.

After that it's entirely up to you but one thing I would suggest is that you stress that all of your estimates are totally free. You should also be prepared to provide some sort of reference example of your work and a website is an excellent showcase of your business.

I certainly don't intend to describe how you should design a website within the constraints of a manual such as this. What I will say though is that believe it or not your domain name is quite important and should reflect what you do. You may also be interested to know that if you decide to set up your site on WordPress, you can also buy a separate domain name and 'point' it at your WordPress site. That means that you don't have to pay a web expert a fortune to design a site. You can use WordPress and you still have the advantage of a .com .org or .net site.

Social Media

Nowadays, it is almost compulsory to have a social media account. If you are able to create an interesting and relevant following, then so much better.

If you have the time to write interesting and informative blogs, you can arrange to have them automatically sent to Twitter or Facebook or LinkedIn or any other social media site you are a member of.

The good thing about social media marketing is that is totally free and if you're lucky you can create a reputation within days rather than months or years.

Your audience on social media is not measured in 'ones and twos' - but in many millions. Just think of the potential.

Nowadays, about 80% of properties have access to the Internet and although social media tends to be the domain of younger people, commerce is fast catching up and there are few companies nowadays who do not have either a Twitter or Facebook account.

Admittedly, the demographic that you may be looking at (for instance the 55+ group) may not all currently be enthusiastic Twitter followers but that is rapidly changing.

I would advise you to open a business Twitter account (it's free) and begin posting. Luckily you are limited to 140 characters so it does not take up all of your time but within your Twitter bio, you can put your contact details and exactly what you do plus you can add a few fictitious or real posts about what you have been doing, issues that you have encountered etc.

It's all about the gradual build-up of an Internet presence because nowadays Google and the Internet in general are the very first port of call for most of the population when looking for goods or services.

There are still some companies who use email for marketing. At this stage all I will say to you is 'Don't'. Unsolicited emails are really not the way to go but eventually when you have built up a reasonable client bank, it is quite correct for you to contact your clients by email in order to remind them that you are still around or to offer discounts etc.

Local Advertising

There was a time when local advertising simply meant a small advertisement in the local newspaper. Although that is still quite useful, as stated above, most people do not read small ads or even go to Yellow Pages. Just to prove a point, have you noticed how Yellow Pages has shrunk in volume over the last five years?

Following on from social media, there are local social media sites or should I say national social media sites which allow you to access a small group of fellow users within your area. That is very well worth looking into because there are quite a few requests for tradespeople on there and I know from personal experience that if somebody on the social media site recommends you, then you are very likely to be considered for a particular contract above someone for instance who has paid for a small ad in a magazine or newspaper. That is how important local social media is as it continues to grow.

Having said all that, local newspapers and magazines still do have their use and if you play your cards right them can be a source of free advertising for you. For instance, if you contact your local newspaper with a reasonably interesting 'human interest' article or story, you will not be ignored.

Local journalists are always hungry for local copy and if, for example, you called your local newspaper and said that you were doing some work for an elderly gentleman who you discovered to have been say a war hero and so you decided to do all the work for free, it is almost guaranteed that a local reporter will show up for an interview.

I'm by no means suggesting that you can do this sort of thing very often, but do keep your eyes and ears open for such possibilities and opportunities.

Apart from local newspapers and magazines, there are parish magazines, club magazines and various other publications with small circulations which tend to be read by the sort of people that will make good potential clients for you. A lot of these magazines are in need of funds and you'll be surprised how cheaply you can advertise in them. It is a good idea therefore to ask around and have a look around and find out what other informal publications there are in your area.

Drop Cards and Pamphlets

Single sheet flyers are one way of actually getting your name and contact details around the area but there will come a time when you realise that the law of diminishing returns has kicked in and the responses you're getting from your flyers aren't what they used to be. This may be a good time for you to think about going slightly upmarket and looking at properly printed and produced pamphlets which will not only give details of your business but will also help you to generate that corporate image that most of us aspire to because that is when the business really starts rolling in.

Well established companies give away pamphlets to potential clients and in the main they are subtle enough not to ask for business but they may contain technical information on a whole variety of subjects.

In your line of business, you may publish a pamphlet which tells potential clients all about grass and how to turf the law and what should be done to a lawn to keep it healthy. If you make a pamphlet interesting enough, and your or your company's details are somewhere on the pamphlet, you will find that people will come to you for further advice, not as readers but as potential clients.

There is a mass of information on the Internet so it is not difficult to write a pamphlet. It does not have to be long and neither does it have to be like a marketing document.

If it is submitted in a cool, informative way without having the immediate appearance of trying to sell something and more importantly it is useful to the potential client, you will find this a very effective way of subliminal marketing.

Whereas a flyer is designed to get your name out there, a pamphlet is a far more subtle way of approaching prospective clients.

For instance, you may choose to have a set of say half a dozen pamphlets, each on a specific subject relevant to the work you do and you can occasionally distribute them to current as well as potential clients. You may be surprised at the responses you get.

Here's an idea for a drop card which worked for me: the idea is similar to a pamphlet but what I did was simply to write a short paragraph introducing myself and my business and the fact that we had recently expanded into the area. There followed a checklist with tick boxes of the services that we were offering and I asked the prospective client to simply tick a box, indicating what sort of work they anticipated they might need doing, a box to add their name and address and a prepaid envelope to return the drop cards to me.

It was a very non-threatening campaign and the response was far better than random distributions.

The secret in all of the above is to keep your eyes and ears open and to be creative, think out of the box and imagine things that your competition would never dream of!

Step 5 – Customers

What Kind of Accounts?

Let's face it, without customers we don't have a business. Therefore it is very important that we try and establish who it is that we want to sell our services to. The process is not random and it is important that you decide at the outset who exactly you want to be distributing to.

There are distinct groups to whom you will definitely not sell lawn care services. For example, a young couple who have just acquired their first property will be very keen to do their own gardening and create their own 'nest'. On the other hand, the affluent baby boomers who have retired early, have a bad back and like to go on holiday five times a year, are ideal clients.

Individuals who rent their properties aren't always interested in the garden and certainly not the lawn but on the other hand people who live in a small block of flats very often have joint responsibility for the upkeep of their communal garden, probably have a committee to organise the work and are therefore prime prospective customers for you.

Purely as an aside, never make the assumption that somebody has thought of something before you. Whether or not you like it, a large part of your job is now sales. Some would say that it is possibly the most important part of your job because without customers your business will die very quickly.

That means that your creative thinking should extend to spotting opportunities in places where others may not see them. For instance, you may assume that your local park is the responsibility of the local authority and that they probably have their own mowers and gardeners – and they probably do. But nowadays with cost-cutting and public bodies being very cost conscious, the likelihood is that all of their work is sub-contracted. A major opportunity for you.

Real estate agents sell properties on behalf of clients. Very often the property is sitting in gardens don't look their best. How about leaving your contact details with local real estate agents? In fact wherever you see a 'for sale' board, either knock on the door or push a flyer or pamphlet through the letterbox.

The possibilities for you are endless and only limited by your imagination, daring and the willingness to expose yourself to the risk of being successful!

Getting First Customers

You will never ever forget your first customer and you will probably do the very best job that you ever do in your life... plus you will enjoy your very first payment more than any other.

As mentioned above, one of the big aspects of your job, certainly at the beginning of your lawn care career is going to be that of salesmen. One of the biggest problems that salespeople have and the reason most of them fail (yes!) is that one of the great difficulties that you will discover is not having the ability to deal with rejection.

When you ask the client whether you can do a job for them, you are quite likely to be in competition with someone else. If a potential client likes you, he will hire you even if your estimate may be slightly higher. It's all about dealing with people.

Personally I found that the easiest marketplace to break into was the elderly market and they are very easily spotted in my area because of the rundown houses and the overgrown gardens. You will find yourself making wrong assumptions at the very beginning. When you see a garden or lawn in very bad condition and unpainted windows in the house you will assume that the person living in there does not have the means to either paint or to tend the garden.

All of us have made the same mistake.

One word of caution. Dealing with an elderly family or person, does not give you a licence to rip them off. If you're kind to them and charge a reasonable amount, you may find yourself being recommended to others in a similar situation.

First customers could be generated as a result of you going to some sort of club and giving a talk on lawn care and gardening in general. I have done that and found it a very lucrative source of business, especially in the early days. Once again, it is something that many people in your position would think about but never actually do.

Always carry your business cards around with you and leave them behind at every possible opportunity.

What Is Your Target Demographic?

Contrary to popular thought, your target demographic is everyone with a garden or a lawn. If they have got a lawn you can look after it. If they haven't got a lawn you can create one for them.

However when we talk about our target demographic we are referring of course to the people we are most likely to get business from.

Let me explain, If you are a young gardener let's say in your 20s or 30s, you are far more likely to relate to people within your age group. If you are starting this business in your 40s and 50s, you will have that credibility which comes with age which will make the retiree and over 50s market much easier to penetrate. Nothing wrong with that, it's just that instinctively, older people will feel more at home with you and less threatened by you. Unfortunately that is human nature.

Moving slightly away from the idea of demographic, I would seriously counsel you to think very hard about anything which is vaguely commercial and which has a garden or a lawn.

For instance I have installed lawns which were owned publicly, replacing masses of flowerbeds which were becoming more and more expensive to maintain. The upshot is that I not only installed quite a bit of lawn but I now have a regular contract maintaining it. All that took a lot of knowledge and a single meeting.

There are many gardening type manuals or books which will list the sort of people that are your target demographic. But once again the secret is in using your imagination.

If you see a new development being built, as soon as the first spade is on the ground, you should have the site managers name so that you can get in front of him and ask whether you can price up the installation of grass and anything else related to the gardens.

Many properties are now being built on spec by builders who may have bought the land a few years ago. They build small little cul-de-sacs or estates, landscape them, build houses and sell them. Call that a demographic or whatever you want but I assure you it is a source of great business.

If you become a real lawn care expert, you may even find yourself being hired as a consultant to a string of golf courses. I know a couple of such people and they make a very nice living on a permanent retainer to a company which owns golf courses.

So don't be narrow minded about who you can sell your services to because believe it or not, the sky *is* the limit.

Referrals

If you have ever been in sales you will understand why I have included a small section on referrals. It is one of those things that every single business and salesperson knows about and in my experience probably less than 1% of them even bother to ask for referrals… again it is because they don't want to mess up their own sale or ruin an imaginary relationship but most of all it's that old 'fear of rejection'.

Asking for referrals is simply asking a satisfied client whether he or she knows of anybody else who could use your services. You should be doing this every single time you complete a job. Don't let your natural reticence and shyness get in the way – just ask. You won't offend anyone… unless of course you're not confident that you did a proper job for your customer.

There is no right or wrong time to ask for referrals, but one of the things that does help is that while you're on site and possibly seeing the client every day, you should be forming some sort of relationship with them. You certainly are going to be getting to know them better and if you're having a drink with them say one morning you could introduce the idea of referrals by saying something along the lines of: *" As you can imagine I don't do much advertising because I just don't have the time. I tend to work on recommendation so when we've finished here, I really would appreciate it if you could think of any people you know that may want similar work doing."*

You plant the seed in their mind, and when you are about to complete the job ask them again and you can refer to that previous conversation. It's very straightforward. You won't always get a recommendation but if you never ask you will *never* get a recommendation – except in very rare circumstances.

And remember, if someone says 'no' to you, it is not an insult and neither is it the end of the world. Just ask!

Step 6 – Manage Business

Book-keeping – SAGE etc.

I think that we have more or less established that lawn care is not going to take up 100% of your time. What with the ordering, the selling, the marketing etc. you'll be very lucky if you spend half your time anywhere near a lawn! But unfortunately there's yet more to think about. Yes it's the dreaded accounting.

Earlier I mentioned that most people whose businesses fail, do so as a result of not seeing enough people, that is to say not acquiring enough new customers. The others get into trouble through either a total lack of accounting or at best a very dubious approach to accounting.

Accounting in its simplest form is a list of your expenditure and a list of your income. You add the items in both columns and then subtract one column from the other. That should tell you whether or not you making any money!

Unfortunately, it is not quite as simple as that and that's why we need bookkeeping, software and accountants.

At the beginning of any new venture, you may think that you are not going to need to do much in the way of accounting but I would suggest that you begin straight away so that you develop proper habits so that when your income is measured in hundreds of thousands or possibly millions, you are already in the accounting groove.

There are many fine books on accounting which will tell you what you can offset against your income but personally I would recommend that you invest in some sort of software. You can see SAGE in the title of this section. SAGE is a very well-known accounting package and an excellent investment for any business – believe it or not I'm not even sponsored by them!

Seriously though, do invest in some sort of accounting package. It'll take care of everything from purchases, income, taxation returns and even everything to do with employees.

A good accounting package can take you from start-up to world domination!

Finally, I would seriously recommend that you talk to an accountant after, say six months of operating. They are not as expensive as you might think and if you have any sort of accounts package which makes the job easier they can create the proper returns for the tax authorities. They will also be able to advise as to whether or not you're making any money.

Incidentally, an accountant's worst nightmare is a self-employed person arriving at their office with a bag of invoices and receipts which is placed on their desk for them to sort out and create accounts. That is when accountants become expensive!

My suggestion is that you get yourself into the habit of obviously keeping all your invoices and receipts, in fact all income and expenditure, and enter them somewhere on a regular basis. Some people do it daily some people do it weekly. The important thing is to discover a routine that suits you and stick to it.

Employees

If you are at the very beginning of your lawn care business career, my initial recommendation to you is don't employ anyone. It is a massive overhead and unless you have contracts ready for the next two or three years, you will be able to manage by hiring somebody on an occasional basis.

Incidentally, many jurisdictions will allow you to put a figure in your accounts in order to pay someone like your wife or close relative to carry out some of your admin duties such as the accounting but again that's one of those things which you will have to investigate, depending on where you are.

If you have somebody working for you who you consider to be self-employed and you show him in your accounts as a straightforward amount of cash every week or every month, beware. If that person works for you for any length of time and you provide him with tools transport etc. you may find the taxation authorities refusing to consider him to be a bona fide self-employed person – especially if for all intents and purposes they are an actual employee who takes care of his or her own tax.

I've only mention the law of diminishing returns once in this manual and if you have never employed anyone else before, don't imagine for one minute that if you employee say three people you are going to make three times as much money. The law of diminishing returns kicks in with a vengeance especially if you get to say ten employees which is when you need to hire a dedicated IT person and a personnel officer. It all depends whether you want to go down that particular route.

I happen to have an acquaintance who is registered as a sole trader rather than a limited company and yet has about 60 people working for him.

I repeat my advice, right at the very beginning if quoting for a job where you feel that you need additional people, use subcontractors and specialists and build their cost into your estimate.

The pitfalls with employees range from providing them with a pension to health and safety issues etc.'

To begin with, keep it simple.

Taxes and Making Provision for Taxes

In most restrictions, you'll be off the taxation authorities' radar for about a year, maybe two years maximum. At the end of that period, you are quite likely to be asked to pay some form of tax.

You may not be surprised to hear that many other businesses fail because they have made no provision for tax and find themselves being bankrupted by the authorities for non-payment.

If you have come from an employed job, taxation is one of those things that you have never had to worry about because it automatically disappears from your pay check every month and you probably don't even know how much it is.

All that changes when you become self-employed and as a rule of thumb approximately 25% of your net income does not belong to you. You should put it aside in a separate bank account ready to hand over to the taxman when the time comes. Always make provision for tax. Talk to your accountant or have a careful look at your accounting software. Either will tell you roughly how much you need to set aside for future taxation liabilities.

When you are new to being self-employed, you're very likely to think that you are far better off than you are in actual fact, and that money you've set aside for taxes will remain very tempting. Leave it alone.

A good accountant will help you to pay as little tax as is legally possible and will produce what is called a profit and loss account statement and all the other bits and pieces that are part of the accounting mysteries which I have never claimed to fully understand or even be interested in.

An accountant would also help you to mitigate your taxation by for instance taking some of your net profit and investing it in a pension which will bring your net income down. That doesn't feel as bad as giving all your money to the taxman.

If you're not sure where to look for an accountant, ask your bank or someone in a similar line of business for a recommendation. That gives you a decent chance of finding an accountant who is not a bandit.

Personal Liability Insurance

First of all, liability insurance is exactly what it suggests in the title. It is always well worth having and in some jurisdictions it will be compulsory. PL insurance will protect you from injury to yourself and to others as well as damage to property.

If you, for instance, are mowing someone's grass and the blade flies off your mower killing your client's dog or smashing his greenhouse, it is a good idea to have the comfort of personal liability insurance to take care of any bills which may occur.

Usually everything from injury cover to legal cover is included and surprisingly it is not as expensive as you might think. As I suggested earlier the best way forward is either to go online and shop around or contact a reputable insurance broker.

The odds are that you will never need your PL insurance and you may think therefore that it is a waste of money right until the moment when that blade flies of your mower or you dig through an electric cable under the grass.

Personal liability insurance should not be optional to you. Build it into your annual budget. The annual premium will be measured in hundreds, giving you coverage measured in hundreds of thousands or millions.

I have already mentioned different types of insurances for insuring your vehicle and your equipment which are 100% necessary whereas other specialist insurances such as business interruption (which is where you are unable to work because of injury etc.) are optional and depend on how much cash you have in hand. However, they can be quite expensive. For the moment other specialist insurance, such as a contract specifically designed to compensate workers from injury, should be on the back burner until you are an employer. However if you do employ someone on a casual basis, do make sure that they understand that any injuries etc. are not your liability.

If you ask them to sign some form of disclaimer to that effect, it may not help as far as any litigation is concerned but it will give you some level of comfort and make the casual employee more careful.

Once again, the best advice would be from your accountant as he will be able to tell you not only what kind of insurance you need but more importantly, what you can afford.

VAT Registration

Value-added tax, TVA, purchase tax or whatever it is called in your particular jurisdiction, is no more than an additional tax that you charge your clients as a percentage of the work you've completed and then once a month, you send the amount you have collected to the tax authorities. It is a tax on goods sold and services rendered. The amount varies from country to country, but on average it is about 20% of your invoice.

The good news is that as a new entrepreneur, in most jurisdictions you are not required to register or collect any type of tax until your net profit or income reaches a certain minimum threshold. For instance in the UK it is currently over £80,000 per year.

Theoretically therefore it is not something you need to worry about at the outset but it is something to bear in mind because once you reach a certain threshold, you become less competitive because you have to add an automatic 20% to your invoice.

Make the most of your early years because you will never be as competitive as that ever again.

I know that some people register for this tax automatically because it makes clients imagine that they are of a certain size and turnover but you have to make the decision as to whether or not you are willing to become what is essentially a tax collector at the same time as making yourself slightly less competitive.

Chasing Payments and Making Refunds

Both of the items in the above title are one of the less pleasant aspects of working for yourself but unfortunately there will be times when your payment is not made in full, whether it is because your client considers your work to be substandard or whether he just does not want to pay you or even does not have the money to pay you.

Once again one does not wish to be too prescriptive but it is a good idea when you are taking on a reasonably sized job to ask for a deposit even if it is only for materials.

Another great way of avoiding cash flow difficulties is to structure a job in sections and take a pre-agreed stage payment from the client. That's a bit of a win-win situation because the client is not having to part with a large amount of cash all in one go and it helps you with your cash flow. That is the way you should select your client.

Incidentally, there are people in our business who have exactly the same reputation as bricklayers who call themselves builders in that they will take upfront cash from several people, attempt to do 3 jobs at once and find themselves not completing any of them. They do it purely for cash reasons and hopefully you will totally avoid that sort of nonsense even though sometimes it will mean refusing a job, postponing it or even giving it to someone else. It is one of the fastest ways to acquire a really bad reputation.

As far as making refunds is concerned, I have to admit that I have never been in that situation and if something does go wrong (and it will), the very best thing you can do is to carry out remedial work yourself. For instance if you create a lawn for someone and six months later you find that it is dipped and is flooding or retaining too much moisture, then there is obviously something wrong in the construction and therefore you are liable for it.

Hopefully, you will be guaranteeing your work to a certain extent but if your client complains that they've got a flooding lawn for instance, be quite prepared to go and do the work as soon as you can, but also be prepared to negotiate some way of compensation if he wishes another contractor to carry out the work.

To briefly return to chasing clients for outstanding money, there will be times when you have to write off amounts because a client refuses to pay. Unless we're talking vast amounts of money, you will find that the easiest way forward will be for you to write off that amount of rather than become involved in litigation or long correspondence. Put it down to experience and move on.

Open a Business Bank Account

Nowadays, everyone is able to open a business account. In fact it is easier to open a business account than it is to open a personal current-account.

Unlike a personal current account, where the bank will undertake all sorts of checks to see whether you have had credit problems, a business account can be opened by you simply producing a memorandum from your company directors, plus some form of ID, and the registration number of your company. A bank account will be opened for you immediately.

The basic business account does not give you any overdraft and if you do open one please do not ask for an overdraft during your first meeting with the bank. Once again, an accountant will help you with a bank account because he will tend to know the local bankers and also be up-to-date with who has the best deals for new companies and newly self-employed people.

If you do decide to go the corporate route and form a company, you will find that company formation agents can very often offer deals which include the opening of the basic business account. They work on commission and should not only create your company but open a business bank account at the same time.

Earlier we talked about making tax provision and I would suggest that when you open a business bank account you open a deposit account in the company's name and use that for your future taxes.

You don't have to do that, but it does keep everything neat.

Whether you are going to trade as a sole trader, partnership, or a limited company, opening a business bank account is surprisingly easy especially as banks tend not to carry out credit checks, because a credit check against the newly formed company, possibly at a new address is a waste of time.

Speaking of new addresses, if you wish to separate your business from your private life, you can register your company at an address even in another town. Many company formation agents also run a business which provides post office boxes as well as company addresses.

How to Minimise Your Tax Liability

Once again, this is where a good accountant is worth the money or fee you're paying him.

My own approach to minimising my own tax liability was to attempt to book everything I spent to the business, ranging from breakfast, lunch, paper purchases, electricity, clothing... in fact everything I could possibly think of.

Luckily my accountant pointed me in the right direction and explained what I could and could not claim for. For instance I mentioned earlier the fact that if you live in a rented property, you may be able to claim part of the rental because you will be using it for your business some of the time.

All of your business operating expenses will be deductible from your income, including your advertising and setup costs as well as your accountant's fees.

Capital expenditure such as your vehicle and your equipment is usually written out of your accounts over a period of years. That simply means that you don't deduct your initial capital expenses in one go, and in most cases you wouldn't want to, especially in the early years because your capital expenditure may well exceed your income during a time when you wouldn't be paying any tax anyway.

If at the end of year one you are showing a net profit of 20%, you are doing very well indeed. It can be a difficult adjustment to realise that everything you are paid by clients is not *your* 'income'.

It is now your GROSS income and it is only after deductions for business expenses, taxation etc. that you arrive at a figure which is called your NET income - a lot of which you will spend on driving the business forward rather than spending it on yourself!

Minimising your tax liability is a relatively straightforward process and will depend on you learning what is acceptable as a deduction to the tax authorities and what isn't.

Invoicing

I have placed invoicing right at the end of this section on financing taxation because it is probably one of the most pleasurable activities that you will be enjoying as an entrepreneur.

I can only pass on my knowledge and I suggest that to begin with you buy yourself a generic invoice book which can either be pre-printed or do what I did and spend a small amount on a good rubber stamp with all my details on. In general, customers almost expect this type of invoice from a tradesman rather than on printed on immaculate 120gsm vellum posted to them by a secretary.

If you carry your invoice book with you, you are always ready to either produce a receipt or deliver an invoice.

A good practice which I would suggest you adopt is to pre-warn your client that you are going to invoice in a day or so. The very last thing you want to hear is a client saying to you *'Sorry I don't have my cheque book with me'* or *'the wallet with my debit or credit card is the office, can you come back tomorrow?'*

Trust me, if you don't manage your clients properly, you will hear both of those excuses and probably many more. The general rule with invoicing is get your invoice in as soon as you can.

The vast majority of people are straightforward honest people, but you will get the occasional client who had no intention of paying the full amount from the very beginning. These people are very difficult to spot and I'm not going to give you a paragraph or two on how to spot different personality types. Just remember to warn your client you are going to invoice them in the near future so that you minimise any opportunity for excuses.

I have mentioned an invoice book. That does not mean that there's anything wrong with producing beautifully typed invoices. In fact, if you are completing a major job, it is a good idea to itemise everything you've done so that the client can see quite clearly what the material charges are and what the labour charges are. If you have told him right at the very beginning what a job is going to cost, there will be no argument.

There will be occasions when you either ask the client for cash for materials, or a deposit. That will not require a formal invoice so the other little book that you need to keep with you is a receipt book.

Although a cheque does not require a receipt because it is a receipt in itself, it is always a good idea to hand a written receipt to your client... and that is certainly true if you are given a bundle of cash.

The other thing you should seriously think about is to give your client the ability to either pay by card or to transfer money directly to your bank. Nowadays apps are available to facilitate that and if you open a proper business account, you should ask for a facility to accept card payments.

Step 7 – Provide Additional Services

I mentioned earlier that it is inevitable that once you are hired to take care of someone's lawn, you will be expected to be an expert on all sorts of gardening matters – and so you should be!

Below I have listed six of the different types of work you may be asked to undertake and that is apart from all the free consultation about plants etc. which you should also be prepared for. Never refuse this kind of work because let's face it if you don't do it someone else will and they will probably know all about lawns as well.

Fall/Autumn Leaf Clean Up

This is especially important if your demographic is the 55+ group. If you haven't got the correct equipment, clearing a garden of fallen leaves is a very labour-intensive job. Unfortunately, the leaves do not simply fall on the grass where they are comparatively easy to break up or blow away but they also fall into the beds and in between plants so if you are to do a proper job, it will take time.

This particular job reminds me of something else that you can always carry as part of your toolkit and that is a whole pile of waste disposal bags. You realise that is good advice when you clear your first garden of autumn leaves.

If you do not want to do the job with the lawn rake, you can buy a blower/garden vacuum. Usually, these are electrically operated and extremely efficient at clearing the garden.

I have found that a straightforward petrol driven lawnmower, with the cutters set very high, also acts like a garden vacuum and if the lawn is dry, it is a very fast and efficient way of ridding the lawn of leaves.

As far as leaf blowers are concerned, there are many different types and prices starting from as little as about $50 all the way up to several hundred dollars.

Snow Ploughing

I'm not for one moment suggesting that snow ploughing is going to be one of your mainstream activities but it should really be a job that if you are ever asked to do, you should accept the opportunity with both hands.

This type of work is only going to come along when lawn care is definitely out of the question!

If you live in an area that has never seen snow, you may ignore this section but if you live in say North America or northern Europe, snow ploughing or probably more accurately snow removal should certainly be part of your repertoire. That would help you to give an impression of a slightly 'bigger' business if you advertise it as one of your services.

Snow clearance does not require any specialist equipment and I would not expect you to invest in a snow plough or any of the more extreme pieces of equipment but a couple of shovels and a trailer will certainly indicate you're willing to move your clients' snow.

This type of job is well worth mentioning because you have to remember that once you've established a relationship with your client as their lawn care specialist, you will find that anything at all that affects the garden will potentially be your job.

Holiday Lighting

This is quite a difficult topic to advise you on because it inevitably means you up a ladder in the middle of winter trying to fix lighting to a soffit board. Needless to say, there are health and safety implications but once again as this is a job which is designed to make the garden look seasonal, I would suggest that you adopt my own method of dealing with what can potentially be a major problem: Find yourself a specialist or two who will complete all garden electrical work for you, including holiday lighting.

So, whether your client wants a water feature with an electrical pump, permanent garden lighting or twinkly lights straight round the garden and the roof, or even an 8 foot Santa climbing down a chimney, use a specialist.

By all means, let your clients know that you can provide such a service and hire someone else to do it. It is well worth doing because if you ask your specialist electrician to quote for you, then you always have the opportunity to create a small margin for yourself and believe you me there are times during the 'off-season' when it will be useful to keep your cash flow moving.

Disposal of Garden Waste

Unless you're a quantity surveyor, you will be constantly surprised at the volume of garden waste that you produce... but there is one law in gardening and that is that whatever job you do in a garden, there will be waste. That is why it is always well worth planning ahead.

Whether you use a truck or as in my case a large trailer there will be times when you have to dispose of soil, old bricks, broken slabs, trees... I know it has absolutely nothing to do with lawn care but it is a very useful service to be able to supply – especially if you are operating in an urban area.

If you have a regular client 'circuit' - that is to say you visit each garden more than once during the year, one of the first things that you should try to persuade the client to establish – or indeed establish it for them is some sort of compost heap. Selling the idea of a compost heap to a client is the easiest thing, because you are recycling and composting and they can even add food waste to it and eventually they will have free compost to spread around the garden and you will not have to make a trip to the municipal tip every time you mow somebody's grass or dig up their lawn.

Hopefully you are beginning to understand why it is impossible to do your kind of work with a normal family saloon car with some tools in the boot.

Garden waste disposal can be a major big-ticket item if you are completing a large job, especially the sort of work that I'm going to describe in the next section. Always remember to include both time and any disposal fees when you are completing an estimate for a client.

Astroturf, Decking, Paths and Concreting

I have to say right at the outset that I'm not a great fan of Astroturf, but believe it or not since it became widely available, there are people who are very keen on having Astroturf in the garden instead of real grass. I have come across people who also have fake flowers. Whether or not you wish to provide a fake grass service is entirely up to you, but all I will say is that I have managed to stay away from it mostly because the number of times that I have been asked to provide fake grass, I can count on the fingers of one hand.

If you can prepare the ground for a lawn, the preparation for laying what is effectively a green carpet is much the same and I'm not for one moment recommending that you use my technique of affecting a look of total shock and acting like a real purist – so if you do lay any Astroturf for a client, remember just one thing, he or you are not going to do much mowing!

Decking first arrived on the scene big-time about 20 years ago and was considered to be the most fashionable way of quickly producing a hard wearing utilitarian surface for both work and play. Nowadays they call it the 'extra room' in the house where people sit, drink, and barbecue. I have constructed many decks and it is a very straightforward process which you can learn by yourself. I would suggest that you do what I did which is to have a look on YouTube and you will be an expert in no time at all!

Paths and concreting are two more standard jobs which you need to get under your belt because if you lay a lawn, the odds are that someone will want a path around it or through it and it is not the sort of job which you should ask another contractor to do. Once again it is a very straightforward task which just means that you have to add other tools to your toolkit such as a builder's spirit level etc. Don't invest in a concrete mixer, (they can be hired very cheaply) although nowadays there are some very reasonably priced electrically driven mixers if you have the storage space.

Supplying Garden Buildings, Tools etc.

Trust me, it won't be very long before you move from pure lawn care to being an overall gardener and garden expert.

The title of this section is about supplying garden buildings etc. but there will be times when you will be asked to not only supply but to erect a garden shed or workshop and once again these are very straightforward jobs which you will gradually acquire. When you first estimate for putting up a shed for instance, *overestimate* the amount of time that you think it's going to take you. That is because no matter how quickly you think you can do the job, it will take you longer.

The reason why you should think about being able to supply tools as well as outbuildings etc. is purely because there's always some margin to be found. If you open an account with a single supplier there will be trade discounts for you which are there for you to create the profit margin rather than to pass on to your client although you're quite at liberty to discount if you wish to do so.

While you're learning all about lawn care, it is also a good idea for you to learn about fencing, building walls, landscaping, building steps, building gazebos, putting together a pergola etc.

My own experience has taught me never to turn down *any* garden-related job. Any job such as building large walls, I do not undertake myself but I know somebody who will and who will also allow me to find a little profit margin for myself.

So once you have established yourself as the lawn care expert, you will soon find yourself being an all-round horticultural expert.

Conclusion

Becoming a lawn care entrepreneur is one of the most rewarding and fastest ways to create not only a client base but to build a successful business.

As you probably gather from what I have written above – lawn care is also a great opportunity to 'branch out' into other aspects of horticulture and once you have established a good reputation, you will have work for the rest of your life.

As your business grows you will learn all aspects of running a business, from accounting, your own motivation, managing people, learning that reward is in direct proportion to effort, buying, selling as well as expanding your circle of friends.

Anything to do with gardening is one of those services where a client is actually letting you into his or her personal life. For instance all of my clients know me by my first name as I do them.

Potentially, every single one of your clients is a client for life and there aren't too many businesses which can actually claim that.

However, please do not go away with the impression that starting any business is easy. If you contact enough people whether directly or through advertising and convert those contacts into customers *and keep doing it* you cannot fail.

Good luck in your new venture, and do let me know how you are progressing.

52688169R00052

Made in the USA
Lexington, KY
07 June 2016